DATE DUE			

Look

....What do you see?

Library of Congress Cataloging-in-Publication Data

Rye, Jennifer.
  Look...what do you see? / Jennifer Rye; illustrated by Tony
Kerins.
    p.   cm.—(First science)
  Summary: Discusses how animals and people use their eyes in
different ways to react to the world around them.
  ISBN 0-8167-2122-X (lib. bdg.)   ISBN 0-8167-2123-8 (pbk.)
  1. Vision—Juvenile literature. [1. Vision.] I. Kerins, Tony,
ill. II. Title.
QP475.7.R94 1991
591.1'823—dc20   90-40231

Published by Troll Associates, Mahwah, New Jersey 07430

Printed in the U.S.A.

10 9 8 7 6 5 4 3 2 1

Look

....What do you see?

Written by
Jennifer Rye

Illustrated by
Anthony Kerins

Troll Associates

Stretch your arms
as wide as you can.
Then look straight ahead.
You can't see your hands, can you?
Remember, don't move your
head or your eyes.
Now move your hands forward slowly,
and very soon they will come into view.

You can see things out of
the corner of your eye,
as you've just seen your hands.
People can see ahead and to the side,
but not behind, without turning
their heads.

Cats' eyes are at the front like ours,
so they can see straight ahead
and to the side.

Rabbits have eyes at the
sides of their heads.
Rabbits can see behind them
without turning their heads.

It's hard to creep up
on a rabbit without being spotted.
Cats are good at hunting,
but rabbits are good at escaping.

We need two eyes for seeing.
With one eye closed, it is hard to guess
how far away something is.
Close one eye. Stretch out your arms
and try to make two pencils
meet in front of you.
Try again, using both eyes.
Which is better, one eye or two eyes?

Try to catch a ball
with one eye closed.

Without your brain, you would not
know what you are looking at.
So seeing is looking at something
with your eyes and
recognizing it with your brain.

This boy is looking at the car.
His eyes send a picture
of the car to his brain.
His brain tells him what it is.

car

Things look fuzzy to a new baby.
Often he smiles at faces,
and other round things
that look like faces.
He keeps looking at things
until he starts to recognize them.
You know that he recognizes things
from his smiles.

Things look fuzzy because he
has not learned to focus his eyes.
Focus means being able to see
near you and far away.

Oh, she's lucky! She's looking
through a telescope.
What can she see that we can't?
What's that on the horizon?
It looks like a blob.
It's fuzzy at first.
Then she focuses the telescope
on the blob. It's a huge tanker,
with a flag flying at the mast.

The telescope makes things
look much bigger.

Now get a magnifying glass and
look at a picture in the newspaper.
The picture is made of
thousands of tiny dots.
Who is that with a spotty face?

Look at a colored picture
in this book. It has dots too.

A magnifying glass makes things
look bigger, but not as big
as a telescope does.

Some animals have eyes that
work like a telescope.
Birds of prey catch and eat
small creatures.
They have a small part of their eye
which can focus at a distance.

A kestrel can spot a tiny
movement in the grass
5,000 feet below.
Then it swoops down very fast
to catch the mouse.

If you can see distant things
very clearly,
but things near you seem blurred,
you are farsighted.
Eyeglasses make things clearer.
Farsighted people need glasses
to see things close up,
like words in a book.

No, they won't work for your eyes.

Nearsighted people need glasses
to see things far away.
Glasses and lenses are made
just for the person who wears them.

Glasses can make things
seem different colors too.
People wear dark glasses to keep
strong sunlight out of their eyes.
Have you ever worn sunglasses?

You can make things seem
different by looking at them
through clear colored paper.
Try looking at a green apple
through red paper.
What color is it now?

When you go swimming,
it's hard to see clearly under water.
Some people wear face masks or goggles.
Fish don't need goggles.
Their eyes can focus in water.

Some flat fish,
which lie at the bottom of the sea,
have both eyes on the top of their head.
They need both eyes to
look out for food.

It is hard to see this fish,
because it matches the stones.

These frogs match their pond water.
They are hiding from the heron,
who would like to eat them.

Animals which match their
background are hard to see.
They are camouflaged.
Their enemies cannot see them,
unless the animals move.
This frog is lying in wait
to catch its dinner of flies.

Deep down in the sea it is quite dark.
Some fish which live there are blind.
Others have very large eyes,
which can see with hardly any light.
One has lights on its teeth
to attract its prey!

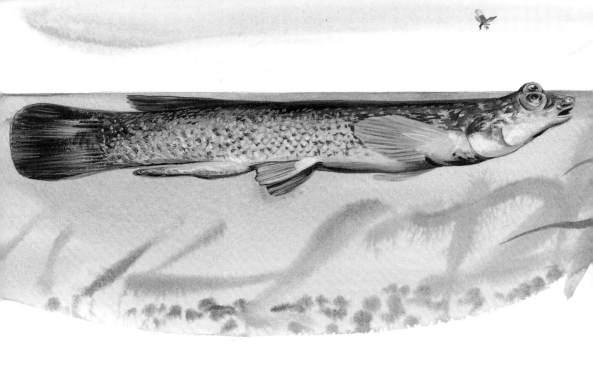

This fish has eyes
that can focus up and down.
It is a good hunter because
of its double eyesight.

WHAT DO YOU SEE? TEST YOURSELF.

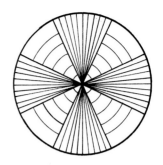

1) Is it two faces looking at each other? Or a vase?

2) Do you see a cross like this + ? Or like this ✕ ?

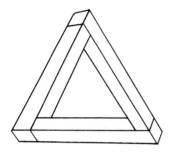

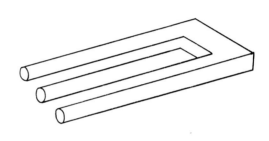

3) An impossible triangle.

4) An impossible fork. Can you draw the triangle and the fork?

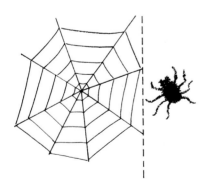

5) Hold a card upright on the dotted line. Bring your face down, and watch the spider move into the web.

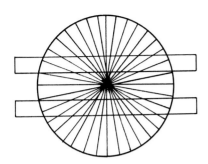

6) Do these rectangles bend in the middle? Measure them and see.

7) Is this a pretty girl or an old woman? Keep staring and you will see both.

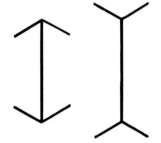

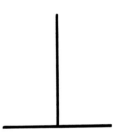

8) Which upright line is longer?

Which horizontal line is longer?

Which line is longer?

9) Prop the book up. Stand a glass of water in front of the arrow, and look at the arrow through the water. It will point the other way.

Your eyes tell you about the color of your clothes, the shapes of flowers and leaves, and the beautiful patterns on a butterfly's wing. Your eyes help you learn. They are your windows on the world.